KT-161-398

101 Things
I Wish I'd Known
Before I Moved House

*Thoughts from those who have
been through it themselves*

Edited by Jane Asher

Illustrated by Rowan Barnes-Murphy

MICHAEL JOSEPH
LONDON

MICHAEL JOSEPH LTD

Published by the Penguin Group
Penguin Books Ltd, 27 Wrights Lane, London w8 5tz, England
Penguin Books USA Inc., 375 Hudson Street, New York, New York 10014, USA
Penguin Books Australia Ltd, Ringwood, Victoria, Australia
Penguin Books Canada Ltd, 10 Alcorn Avenue, Toronto, Ontario, Canada m4v 3b2
Penguin Books (NZ) Ltd, 182–190 Wairau Road, Auckland 10, New Zealand

Penguin Books Ltd, Registered Offices: Harmondsworth, Middlesex, England

First published 1996
10 9 8 7 6 5 4 3 2 1

Copyright © Jane Asher, 1996
Illustrations copyright © Rowan Barnes-Murphy, 1996

The moral right of the editor has been asserted

All rights reserved. Without limiting the rights under copyright reserved above, no
part of this publication may be reproduced, stored in or introduced into a retrieval
system, or transmitted, in any form or by any means (electronic, mechanical,
photocopying, recording or otherwise), without the prior written permission of
both the copyright owner and the above publisher of this book

Set in 11/15pt Monotype Baskerville
Designed in QuarkXpress on an Apple Macintosh
Printed and bound in Great Britain by BPC Hazell Books Ltd
a member of the British Printing Company Ltd

A CIP catalogue record for this book is available from the British Library

ISBN 0 7181 3966 6

I have been lucky enough to receive observations on the traumatic business of moving house from many people. Among them I would particularly like to thank: Ygal Giramberk, Anji Loman-Field, Peter Mills, Margaret Ousby, Jane Struthers, Eric Schneider, Anita Chisholm, Danielle Fluer, Mike Emery, Tika Cope, Kim Fuller, Mark Redhead, Helen Soffa, Gavin Hunter, Susan Ben-Bassett, Sarah Hill, Maryon Tysoe, Adrian Silas, Christopher Wilson, Anne Breen, Sophie Tsiu, Doreen Halper.

And my grateful thanks to Rowan Barnes-Murphy for his delightful illustrations.

INTRODUCTION

Moving house comes very high on the list of stressful events and as soon as the subject is mentioned in company someone will volunteer a ghastly story about a survey, a gazumping, a builder, a solicitor or some removal men. But, equally, few things produce as much happiness as a successful change of home. Moving into one's dream house for the first time, or moving away from home into one's own flat can be immensely satisfying and exciting.

For those about to go through the joys and traumas of a move, I have gathered together some thoughts, experiences and pieces of advice from those who have either been through it recently, or are seasoned movers.

Some of their stories are funny, some are horrific and some are simply practical, but I do hope that for those of you about to take the plunge and uproot yourselves, you may find a glance through these pages entertaining as you perch on a packing case and sip that well-deserved cup of tea. *Jane Asher*

1 ... not to take out such a huge mortgage. Signing a piece of paper which makes you owe more than a hundred times the amount of money you've ever had is scary. But all my friends were saying, 'Borrow to the hilt! Get the biggest mortgage they'll give you!' Well, that was in the Eighties, when by the time you'd finished breakfast your house's value had increased by 30 per cent. Shame none of my friends was clairvoyant.

32-year-old man, moved twice

... not to get emotionally attached to a house until you've paid for it. The moment I saw our second house I could visualize us living there, and it just seemed so right. I fell in love with it, which is a bad thing to do, as it makes negotiations really difficult. I know I ended up paying far too much.

38-year-old woman, moved twice

... to check that all bills have been paid on a house before you take it over. Two days after I moved in I was presented with a writ. A builder who had done work for the previous owner hadn't been paid. I had to sue the solicitor who'd done the conveyancing and the previous owner. Eventually we settled out of court, but it certainly took the edge off owning the perfect home.

Married couple, moved once

4 ... that you should move house in California. They really know how to do it. You wake up in your old house with everything as usual: fridge full of food, clothes in the wardrobes, dirty pots and pans in the sink, ashtrays full of butts. You know, normal house. Then the movers come, and two hours later the house is an empty shell. In the afternoon you drive to your new house – and everything is there, unpacked and in its place! Of course, you have to move the potted plants to a better corner and find that the stereo hasn't been properly rewired, but it's minor stuff. Amazing. It's worth living in California just for that!

40-year-old man, moved several times

5   ... to spend a night in your new house, if you possibly can, before buying it. Each house has a different character depending on what time it is, and sometimes you hear really strange noises at night that you were quite unaware of during the day. And even if it is quiet, some houses can be spooky. You'll be spending a third of your life in it at night, and you should know what it's like before plonking down the dosh.

29-year-old man,
moved several times

... to be very wary of prospective vendors who seem reluctant to make an appointment for you to view the house in the evening, after dark. It's likely to mean that you'll need to rewire the premises.

30-year-old woman, moved twice

7 ... to beware strong smells and evocative whiffs when being taken round a house you're thinking of buying. The smell of freshly brewed coffee could well be covering the smell of freshly mouldering damp.

28-year-old woman, moved several times

... that once the basic price is agreed, you should firm up on every detail about fixtures and fittings. Itemize them. Assume nothing. We once moved into a house where the previous owners had actually removed all the light bulbs, door knobs, door hooks and even the front-door lock. It's also a good idea to agree not just a date but a time to complete. When we moved the vendors assumed they had until midnight to leave. Of course, they needed the extra time – they were very busy taking everything that could be removed.

28-year-old woman, moved several times

... to keep pets well out of the way. They can get very stressed during the course of a move. Next time I'll be much more careful and make sure our dog Becks doesn't witness the packing. For a year and a half after the move Becks had colitis, which, according to the vet, was a direct result of stress associated with the move.

Woman in her thirties, moved once

10 ... that I should think about the pets' packing as well as our own. My strongest memory of our last move was sitting in the car with a goldfish tank on my lap and driving for 100 miles while worrying whether the fish were going to make it. If only I'd thought it through. Another time I'd put them in a clear plastic bag with three inches of water in it inside a cardboard box – something that would be light to carry and would prevent the fish from knowing where they were going.

50-year-old man,
moved several times

... how emotional I'd feel. The night before you move out of the old home into the new one is a very difficult time. Beside all the worry about the event itself, I couldn't help looking around me and thinking about the experiences I'd had there – the laughs, the tears, the friends, the Christmases – and wondering what was going to happen to me in the new place.

34-year-old woman, moved several times

... that you should supervise the packing of your most precious possessions. When the movers come, follow them round and point out any delicate things. Both times I've moved there have been breakages, and getting the moving company to cough up the insurance is a hassle. By the time you're in the new house and you've restored some order the last thing you need is to fill out lengthy insurance-claim forms.

32-year-old woman, moved twice

... to organize cleaning help. If you can afford it, I'd recommend hiring two cleaners for the day: one in the old house and one in the new.

Married woman with children, moved several times

14   ... to pack one box or container yourself with emergency stuff and take it to the new house. You know: kettle, mugs, tea, kitchen roll, loo roll and a couple of plates for the sandwiches you've prepared. Putting the kettle on will be the first thing you do in the new house. And include a few sweets for the children. It's also a good idea to have all cleaning materials easily accessible because you'll be cleaning as soon as you've drunk that first cup of tea.

42-year-old woman with children, moved several times

15 ... how wonderful I'd feel. Your first owned home is like first love – actually, better. For about three weeks I felt as if I were on holiday: excited, exhilarated and full of the joy of having my own space. The first visitor, the first record played, the first cooked meal – all took on great symbolic significance. In spite of having shared flats before, this was much more of a rite-of-passage thing. I felt adult.

32-year-old man

... to write to the local tax office as soon as the mortgage is agreed and you're ready to exchange contracts. It takes a while to get the readjustment on your income tax, and during the first few months – and usually long after – you really need the extra money.

27-year-old woman, moved once

17 ... that you should never pick either the handsomest or the cheapest when choosing a builder. You'll regret it.

42-year-old woman, moved several times

... that all builders are economical with the truth. They can't help it – it's in their genes. As soon as a builder starts calling you 'love', beware: he is about to tell you a really big porky.

30-year-old woman, moved several times

... that whatever the sum that's been agreed on for building work, you have to add on at least half again. The same goes for time. If the builders say two months, they really mean three. And hold some money back till the end of the job. That's for when they do the invisible man trick and don't turn up for the last bits and pieces.

33-year-old woman, moved twice

... to lock your bedroom door. I moved into a large, unmodernized flat and had to live there during extensive renovation. I camped out in one room, while the builder had a key and used to turn up every morning before I went to work. One morning I woke up to find him sitting on the edge of my bed, holding my hand and telling me, in the sweetest possible way, that I owed him £800 for materials. If I ever find myself in the same situation again, the first thing I'll do is buy the biggest lock I can find and fix it on the bedroom door.

31-year-old woman, moved once

... to shop around for mortgages and conveyancing. There are significant differences in prices. If you don't take the time to research, it costs you.

40-year-old man, moved several times

... to be aware of the positions of local schools when looking for somewhere to live. My first flat was positioned between a junior and a senior high school. The porch was ideally placed for the pupils to have a cigarette between classes. Finding groups of kids, dog-ends, crisp packets and cans on the doorstep was a constant irritant.

32-year-old woman, moved several times

... to bribe professional movers. On moving day the first thing you have to do is make them a cup of tea, and buy a bumper packet of chocolate biscuits to go with the tea. Even more important, tip them. Tipping them in advance makes all the difference to their attitude. Helpful movers can take a lot of the stress out of the day.

Young man, moved once

24 ... to make the new house your own as quickly as possible. After four moves I've worked out how to do it. (This is going to sound very peculiar, I know.) You have to put on your favourite music, get some of your own smells around the place ... and also talk to it. Introduce yourself. Tell the house that you chose it and how happy you hope to be there. Yes, I know it sounds crackers, but it's no more daft than what animals do when they pee around the perimeter of their new territory.

30-year-old woman, moved four times

... that it really is worth hiring professional movers. After my first bachelor-girl flat I was lulled into a false sense of security when my husband and I moved into our first home together. We thought we'd do it all ourselves, so I found myself packing at the last minute – not something I'd recommend. We arrived at the new house after dark, so we missed the electricity man who was going to switch us on, and there were dozens of snails on the front door because of the damp. I thought I'd died and gone to Hell.

42-year-old woman, moved twice

26 ... that you must label everything. You think you'll remember where things are and what is in each box, but you won't. The more labelling you put on boxes and packing cases the better – it pays off hugely in terms of diminished stress levels.

30-year-old woman, moved several times

... that all houses have individual quirks you don't appreciate until you move in. It's a bit like getting to know someone in a new relationship. Our house is really cute. As soon as you pull out a drawer in the kitchen, it comes right out and drops on to your foot.

42-year-old woman, moved several times

... that the first thing you should do when you move in, whatever the weather, is to open all the windows. It's like getting all the old smells out of the place before making it your own.

30-year-old woman, moved several times

29 ... not to order too many change-of-address cards. Better to order too few and send out some extra postcards than be left with a stack of formal cards which have no other use.

42-year-old woman, moved several times

... that a kind gesture can mean a lot. When I moved into my new home I found a welcoming bottle of wine and a box of chocolates had been left for me by the previous owner. I wish I'd thought to do the same in the house I had left.

42-year-old woman, moved twice

31   ... that after you move in there's always a period, a bit like falling out of love, when you notice all the irritating little things about your house – as you do with your partner. Since you've made the commitment, you start turning the house into what you want it to be, and it does eventually become the way you want it. Too bad it's not so simple with a partner!

40-year-old woman,
moved several times

... that you must sort out your priorities when it comes to space. There's a great element of compromise in choosing a home. You are never going to get everything you want, so you have to decide which are the most important issues – the ones you insist on. In my first flat I compromised on the shoe-box kitchen for the big living-room. In my second, I had a decent-sized kitchen but no garden. Now I've got the garden but am back to a small kitchen.

36-year-old woman, moved three times

... that moving is when you find the things you'd lost and are really pleased to see again and also, unfortunately, the things you didn't want to find.

42-year-old woman, moved three times

34 ... that, along with death (probably some-one else's but not necessarily), divorce, changing jobs and getting married, moving is about the most stressful thing you can do.

50-year-old woman, moved several times

... to include everything in your calculations. Every time I've moved and made projections about the cost of the exercise, I've always forgotten the disconnection and reconnection expenses. And they can certainly add up.

40-year-old man, moved several times

36 ... that you should never arrange for building work to be done when you're living in your new property – unless you want the builders to use your best china for the turps and paintbrush cleaning.

50-year-old woman, moved several times

37 ... that household pets always know you're moving long before you do.

28-year-old woman, moved twice

... that there are times when the business of moving seems impossible. There's a really terrible moment when you're in the middle of packing cartons. It seems like an insurmountable task. You think you will never, ever get it done, and you ask yourself how on earth you managed to accumulate all this junk. But somehow, magically, you eventually win through.

58-year-old woman, moved several times

39 ... to get the timing right. There is no feeling like the abject horror and gut-wrenching fear of having exchanged on your present property while you are suffering a major delay in exchanging on the new one.

40-year-old man, moved twice

... that the price of property can go down as well as up. Now, that *was* a nasty surprise!

38-year-old man, moved twice

41 ... not to trust the vendors until you've exchanged. You've shaken hands, gone to dinner, declared lifelong friendship, admired their awful taste, told them that their property will continue to be lovingly maintained in your hands. And then they accept another £500 from a demolition company just as you were about to exchange. You've been gazumped!

Married couple, moved threee times

... to be ready for a depressing survey. The chimney is leaning perilously; there is a crack in the side wall; the property has been erected on a tributary of the Thames; none of the doors has closed properly since 1923; there is a water mark on the inside front wall; a tile from the roof almost stuns the postman. Welcome to the wonderful world of the structural survey. This is the document that says the new home you've set your heart on is a wreck. And it gives 432 reasons why you should never live there but, mysteriously, still confirms that it is worth the asking price.

Married couple, moved several times

43 ... not to rush to move out. Why do prospective buyers always ask if you can move out quickly even though they have no intention of moving in quickly? We made a huge effort to get out of the house as fast as we could, then found that the new owners didn't move in for months.

40-year-old man, moved many times

... to get rid of things before you move, not after. Moving is very expensive and time-consuming, so the less baggage you are travelling with, the more cost-effective the move will be and the easier your arrival in your new home. Set yourself the target of going through one cupboard a day in the weeks leading up to the move, and be ruthless – throw out everything you don't really need.

48-year-old woman, moved several times

... that it's worth taking with you anything that the new owners of your home don't want – carpet, curtains, curtain rods, door handles, light switches, cooker, fridge and so on. You'll be surprised what you can save by taking with you things like these, which can be reused. And if you don't want to reuse them yourself, put an ad in a free sheet – my ad paid my moving bill.

30-year-old man, moved once

46 ... not to use the surveyors from the building society as your own surveyors. They are interested only in securing the money for the loan, not your investment. It's always worth getting a very thorough surveyor's report. Ancient wiring, a faulty heating system, a leaking roof – these things are very expensive to fix, so make sure that you either get the price lowered or decide not to buy.

Married couple, moved three times

... not to overstretch yourself financially to buy a place, however much you love it. If you can't really afford it, it can become your own personal nightmare.

38-year-old man, moved once

... never, ever to buy before you have sold. If you take on a large bridging loan, within a matter a months you could lose any equity you ever had by trying to meet the payments.

Married couple, moved twice

... to live in your new home for a while before you decorate. You will then know what you want and where you want it. Decorating too quickly means that you may do things that need changing a year or so later.

62-year-old woman, moved several times

50 ... that although it goes without saying that you should put your home on the market for a slightly higher price than the amount you want so that you have negotiating power, it's not worth being greedy. You will lose potential buyers.

Couple in their forties, moved several times

... that you should try to negotiate with estate agents over their commissions. Very often they'll drop their price. And if they don't, you haven't lost anything.

50-year-old man, moved several times

52 ... that you should wait for the sales before buying for your new home. You can equip a place for a fraction of the normal cost. It's also worth while going to auctions.

Woman in her thirties, moved twice

... that most of the stress and anxiety comes from not being prepared. Mind you, it's all very well saying don't leave everything until the last minute. We started packing boxes, numbering them, putting loads of details on them. As the number of boxes increased, there were fewer and fewer details on them. Embarrassing to admit, we found the teaspoons six months after moving in.

Married man, two moves

54 ... that during the buying and moving-in process your cheque book is in constant use. I seemed to be writing the same figure for lots of different items. Or perhaps I'd strayed into cheque-book Hell, and it had all become a surreal nightmare.

Married man, one move

... to ask the neighbours about the managing agents if you're thinking of moving into a leasehold flat. If there's any hesitation in their response – don't buy the property. Once I'd moved into my flat I had all sorts of 'maintenance' demands: I'm sure I was being cheated, as they would not produce invoices for work supposedly done. I refused to pay, and they finally took me to court. When the judge said that my only option was to move, I came home and put the flat straight on the market. The experience left a very bad taste in my mouth.

38-year-old woman, moved twice

... how to pick the right area to live in. We spent months looking in all the wrong places, but a friend had just the right idea. He had to move to London for work but didn't have a clue where he should live. He decided that his priority was to be near a park and a tube station. When he'd isolated the areas he could afford he bought a pair of compasses and drew concentric circles around the tube stations and the parks. This meant that there were only a few streets in which to choose property and made the business of wading through estate agents' listings much easier.

Married couple in their thirties

... that neighbours matter. There's a lot of luck involved in acquiring the right ones, and it's worth doing a little investigating before you buy if you possibly can. After several moves we've finally got it right: we're blessed with a house of nuns on one side and a croupier on the other. Not only does this mean that we're comfortably positioned between the spiritual and the temporal; it also means there's someone around during the day when we're at work.

Married couple, moved several times

... to choose a house you like, not one that you think is a good investment. Those days have gone – which is just as well. Buy the house because you want to live there, otherwise you'll spend years wishing you were living somewhere else.

Woman in her sixties

... to ask the previous owners about handymen before they leave. Whenever you move into a new home there are always teething troubles, which usually occur at the most inconvenient times. My heating broke down when the weather was really cold, and I was cursed with the plumber from Hell. He seemed incapable of isolating the problem. He kept coming back with a new idea or another bit of equipment. And each time he'd take off his shirt and bend over the boiler, and I was subjected to plumber's bottom at twelve o'clock at night. Not a pretty sight, I can tell you.

38-year-old woman, moved twice

... that builders can be a serious health hazard. Major renovations in a new home equal major anxiety and stress. The worst day was when the lintel fell through the ceiling and they spilt paint on the carpet. I came home to find the house deserted. It was like the *Marie Celeste*: the front door was wide open and there was chaos inside. I went over to the pub opposite and found the builders having a drink. I suspect they were planning the next stage in the programme to mutilate my home and drive me insane.

Woman in her thirties, moved several times

61 ... never to pay builders by the day. I learnt from bitter experience. As soon as you do they go into slow motion and develop a variety of ills which mean that they have to sit down and drink yet more tea. Also never buy materials for them. You may think you're saving money, but you're not. You don't always have quite the right measurements or quantities, and you spend your life going backwards and forwards, replacing bits and pieces and being landed with useless leftovers.

33-year-old woman, moved
several times

... to be very wary of builders' clever ideas. If you're planning renovations and the builder advises you strongly to do something, don't make an immediate commitment. I got stuck with a system of concealed lighting that was supposed to be wildly economical. It's never worked properly, and I'm convinced it was a job lot the builder wanted to dump on some schmuck.

35-year-old man, moved once

... not to be tempted to accept your friends' kind offers of help with the move. I did – and wouldn't do it again. The agony of wondering if your less-than-fit friend will put his back out is awful, plus the fact that you are indebted for ever. In the end it's a much more expensive option.

38-year-old man, moved twice

64   ... not to unpack your clothes if you're going to be stripping or sanding. Wherever you put them, even in wardrobes, the dust will find them. And if you're doing anything connected with chimneybreasts or floorboards, the quantity of filth flying around will be magically quadrupled.

38-year-old woman

... that there's a mysterious black hole into which precious bits and pieces will disappear each time you move house.

Young woman, moved several times

... how disorientated I would feel. The last time I moved it took me days to get over the feeling of not really knowing where I was. When I came out of my new bedroom in the morning I turned right in the direction of my old kitchen. I'd be several paces down the hall before I realized I was going the wrong way.

Single woman, moved several times

67 ... what 'a little bit of damp' signifies. I didn't realize that this would mean that countless people would be coming to look at it, smell it, touch it, assess it, fix it. At times it felt as though I'd bought an ancient monument.

40-year-old man

68 ... that, however expensive, a full survey is worth it. We thought we couldn't afford one, which in retrospect was a mistake. Our house is built on very deep foundations, and the floorboards were rotted through. This became evident only when my husband took out the sink and it fell through the floor – six feet.

Married couple,
moved once

... that cheap carpet can work wonders. Our new house was a wreck. We had enough money to do a bit of a rewire and to put in heating and a bathroom. It was very difficult having two boys running around on the floorboards. So we did something clever. We bought the very cheapest carpet available and laid it. This made an enormous difference: it kept the dust down.

Married couple in their fifties

70 ... to watch out when you let workmen into your house. When the damp man came he went into the loft and found an old encyclopedia, which he took away to be valued. We never saw him again. And he never sent in his estimate.

Married couple,
moved twice

... to find out about the previous occupants. For the first few months in our new house we were haunted by their ghosts – or at least the shades of their friends and associates. The house was apparently home to a number of prostitutes, so we had some very unusual callers at the front door. It had also been used for storing stolen goods, so the police called round twice. It took a while for the place to lose its reputation as a house of ill repute.

Married woman with two children

... to check on future neighbours. When I bought my flat I had absolutely no way of knowing that I would be living above a liability. The batty old dear nearly blew up the street. I'd only been in the flat three days when I smelt gas coming out of her flat. I tapped on her door, introduced myself and warned her. She wasn't having any of it. She couldn't smell gas, therefore there was no leak. She slammed the door in my face. I tried again. This time she reappeared at her door with a box of matches to prove her point. I pleaded: 'Whatever you do, please don't light that match!' She lit it. I held my breath. Nothing happened. When the emergency services arrived they said that the only reason why the whole street hadn't gone up was because the concentration of gas was too high to ignite. I live in fear!

Young woman, moved once

73 ... to try to view a house when it is as empty as possible – or at least to push things around a bit. When you go to see the house that you want to buy, very often it looks lovely and cosy, with the owners' things scattered around. After they move out you notice the coffee stain on the carpet that was hidden by the sofa and the marks on the walls where they've removed the pictures. The first day is quite a shock.

Woman in her thirties,
moved once

... that it's very important to remember that if you find something damaged or notice missing items after the move, most insurance policies allow you only seven days to inform the removal company and file a complaint. This is a rip-off because, let's face it, it usually takes a lot longer than seven days to get yourself straight, particularly if you're planning major renovations and your stuff is still in boxes.

Man in his forties, moved three times

... to check on the route to your new house. I sent a friend ahead with the keys to the new house while I followed in the removal van. Disaster struck when the van got stuck under a low-level bridge. The traffic was held up, the police arrived and there was total confusion. After an extended detour we eventually arrived at the house just as it was getting dark. Fortunately, my friend had the foresight to rush out and buy cans of beer and bacon sandwiches to spur the men on to finish unloading. A cool head in a crisis is what you need on moving day!

80-year-old woman

... to label the dog as well as the packing cases. Everything seemed to go very well when we moved. My daughter brought the family dog along and introduced him to the new home. She left him in the garden for about five minutes – and suddenly there was no dog. We spent the next four hours looking for him. Needless to say, we hadn't changed the disc on his collar. While we were tramping the streets and driving back to the old house looking for him, we didn't realize that some kind person had found him, fed him and was trying to reach us at the old telephone number, which had been disconnected. If I'd put the new number on his tag, we would have been saved hours of worry.

70-year-old woman, moved three times

77 ... not to forget to have cash ready. We moved on a Saturday morning, and the movers arrived late. They were expecting to be paid in cash. I had to deal with the children and didn't have time to get to a cashpoint. Then I couldn't find my cashcard. When I was on the point of tears my neighbours came round and lent me some money. And that made me want to cry even more because I was losing them.

45-year-old woman, moved once

... not to worry so much. After thirty years working as a teacher in an inner-city area I took my pension and decided to move to the country. For months before I went I was anxious about what I was doing. I've now got a job in a boutique, which I really enjoy: this last year has been the best year of my life. I wish I'd known it was going to be like this – I'd have worried much less.

55-year-old woman

... to be ready for last-minute emergencies. My son had been asking me to come and stay with him in Los Angeles for several years – he didn't like the idea of my living in London on my own. But I had my friends, my independence, my interests and hobbies. Eventually I agreed to go to Los Angeles and put my house on the market. It took a long time to sell, but then a buyer came along who offered the right price. Completion day came. The house was empty. Then I tripped, broke my ankle and had to be taken to hospital. The buyer said that he couldn't proceed, so I had to start all over again. But I must say that when I did leave, I was very pleased to go.

70-year-old woman

... that, if you can, before completion date you should test the equipment that the vendor has agreed to leave behind. We moved in, having bought the previous owner's fridge and cooker, to find that the fridge leaked and only one burner on the cooker worked. By then it was too late. All the vendor said was, '*Caveat emptor,*' which wasn't very helpful.

42-year-old woman, moved three times

81 ... that my car would be stolen as I slept on my first night in my new flat in its lovely posh area. I felt I wanted to move back to the safer and more secure – but less smart – area that I'd lived in before.

29-year-old woman

82 ... to put the zapper for the TV and video within easy reach. When you're surrounded by cardboard boxes and you haven't the energy to search for anything, it certainly helps if you can quickly reprogramme the channels, order take-away pizzas and slump in a heap.

Married couple, moved several times

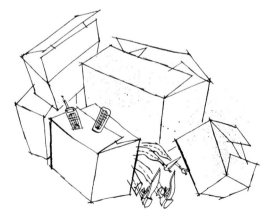

... not to believe what your parents tell you about pets. The first time we moved, from a house to a flat, I was five years old. We had to leave our dog behind, as no pets were allowed, but I believed my parents when they said that Smokie would be sad for a while but would then be happy with his new owners. As it turned out, they were wrong. We went back to see him once. His new owners beat him and starved him and drove him mad. He was frightened and ill and had welts and bald patches all down one side. I tried to talk to him from the next-door neighbour's fence. I remember hoping that they were right about him not remembering me.

46-year-old man

... that when you put things into storage for a planned six months, you should assume they'll be there for a year. Everything takes longer than you think.

25-year-old woman, moved once

... that I would miss my old neighbours. At the time they seemed over-nosy, over-noisy and over-sexed. After I left I realized how comforting I found the predictability of their behaviour!

35-year-old woman

... never, ever to talk directly to the prospective buyers of your house once negotiations have started. It can land you in all sorts of trouble. Much better to let the estate agents handle everything.

48-year-old man, moved several times

... that, if you can, you should splash out and hire a professional cleaning company for one day. They will clean a house from top to bottom. I realized this after spending more than three weeks doing it myself.

Woman, moved twice

... that I wouldn't be able to park my car outside my house ever again.

Married man, moved once

89 ... that four of my customers lived in the same road.

30-year-old man

90   ... that you should check out the garden at different times of the day. I only realized after I moved in that the sun is totally blocked for most of the afternoon by the two trees in the garden.

Married man, moved twice

... not to believe the sellers' descriptions. They made a big deal about the barbecue they were going to leave behind in the garden of my first house. Consequently, while I waited in my flat for completion day I spent many evenings imagining myself in my manicured garden, sipping cold white wine and turning over perfectly barbecued steaks to the amazement of my friends. The reality was a pile of rust. Nice dreams, though!

28-year-old woman, moved once

... how to deal with ash on the carpet. The trick is to accumulate a large enough mass of cigarette ends and ash without any attempt at clearing it up. Once you've built up the pile, you're able to sweep it up.

38-year-old man, moved several times

... that you can keep the same telephone number if you're moving within the same area – and most moves are within a very small radius. And nowadays you don't have to trek round the telephone, electricity and gas offices to get everything transferred: you can arrange it all over the phone.

48-year-old man, moved several times

... what living abroad would really be like. We moved to France three years ago. There were many things I wish I'd known before the event. First of all, when you see all those homes in magazines they never show the way French houses are always painted brown. Every single thing in our house was brown. It was like being buried alive. But that problem was easily solved with white-wash. The other dream that was shattered wasn't so easy to solve. The first day we set ourselves up in the early-morning sunshine to have our breakfast outside, just as we'd imagined it. As I took my first sip of coffee, its aroma mingled with the smell from the nearby pigsty.

Married couple, moved several times

... that, if you hire a Transit van and drive it yourself, you must ensure that everything is securely tied down. If not, when you turn your first corner all your fixtures, fittings and treasured possessions will be smashed beyond recognition. It seems perfectly obvious now, but I had to learn from experience.

30-year-old man

... to be absolutely ruthless about memorabilia. That means throwing away those old Christmas cards, school books, theatre and concert programmes. There is absolutely no point in carting that stuff around. You'll never look at it, and it weighs a ton.

Woman in her seventies

... that when you get to the business of packing, it's a good idea to pack cupboard by cupboard. Generally speaking, in the new house you'll organize things similarly, and you can save yourself a lot of time.

Married woman, moved three times

... that you should start packing the day you decide to move house. By the time you find yourself reading all those old letters you can't part with, the six months or so will have flown by.

55-year-old man, moved several times

99 ... that, if you're moving with children, you should make sure you're one step ahead of them. This means deciding who gets which room and having keys ready for them from day one. When you're stressed out with the rest of the move, you don't need the kids giving you grief as well.

Married man in his fifties

... to put all your favourite plants from the garden into pots before you start showing round prospective buyers. Otherwise you're not allowed to take them with you. And bring all the pots into the house on the day of the move: you don't want disgruntled removal men thinking they've finished, then being shown a lot of heavy pots in the back garden at the last minute.

48-year-old man, moved several times

101 ... that you'll need sheets and towels ready to hand. You'll be exhausted after the move and will probably want to collapse into bed soon after you're in the house. Clean sheets on the beds and fresh towels in the bathroom will make the new house feel like home.

48-year-old woman, moved twice